Wake Up Girl...
AND PUSH THROUGH!®

VOLUME 1

Shantia Coleman

Designate Morning Alone Time With God

TABLE OF CONTENTS

Dedication *1*
Introduction *2*
Day 01 Prayer *5*
Day 02 Prayer *6*
Day 03 Prayer *7*
Day 04 Prayer *8*
Day 05 Prayer *9*
Day 06 Prayer *11*
Day 07 Prayer *12*
Day 08 Prayer *13*
Day 09 Prayer *14*
Day 10 Prayer *15*
Day 11 Prayer *17*
Day 12 Prayer *18*
Day 13 Prayer *19*
Day 14 Prayer *20*
Day 15 Prayer *21*
Day 16 Prayer *23*
Day 17 Prayer *24*
Day 18 Prayer *25*
Day 19 Prayer *26*
Day 20 Prayer *27*
Day 21 Prayer *29*
Day 22 Prayer *30*
Day 23 Prayer *31*
Day 24 Prayer *32*
Day 25 Prayer *33*
Day 26 Prayer *35*

Wake Up Girl and PUSH Through!

Day 27 Prayer *36*
Day 28 Prayer *37*
Day 29 Prayer *38*
Day 30 Prayer *39*
Day 31 Prayer *41*
Day 32 Prayer *42*
Day 33 Prayer *43*
Day 34 Prayer *44*
Day 35 Prayer *45*
Day 36 Prayer *47*
Day 37 Prayer *48*
Day 38 Prayer *49*
Day 39 Prayer *50*
Day 40 Prayer *51*
Day 41 Prayer *53*
Day 42 Prayer *54*
Day 43 Prayer *55*
Day 44 Prayer *56*
Day 45 Prayer *57*
Day 46 Prayer *59*
Day 47 Prayer *60*
Day 48 Prayer *61*
Day 49 Prayer *62*
Day 50 Prayer *63*
Let's Stay Connected *64*
Books by Shantia *65*

DEDICATION

This book is dedicated to Shareka Jones, my one and only sister. The sudden loss of her pushed me to find meaning in life which led me down a spiritual journey of seeking God and developing a personal relationship with Him. Shareka, I miss you dearly and I know that you would be my biggest cheerleader and supporter for how God is using me to encourage and uplift other women with tools and resources that helped *me* make it through! Girl, I love you and I know you are proud!

ISBN Paperback: 978-1-7372777-0-5
ISBN eBook: 978-1-7372777-1-2
©2020 All Rights Reserved. No part of this document may be reproduced or transmitted in any form or by any means, electronic to mechanical- including photocopying recording or by many information storage and retrieval system-without written consent from the author.

INTRODUCTION

I've been searching for words to express how truly powerful it is to "Designate Morning Alone Time With God" and the two words that I can think of to describe this amazing feeling is - "Life-Changing." Because every morning that I spend time with God is changing my life from the *inside-out*.

Life is all about making choices, and I've learned that some choices we make are easier than others. The name of this book and the inspiration for writing it was birth from a personal choice that I make every day when I set my alarm clock to wake up at 4:30 A.M. While my eyes are still closed, and I'm getting out of the bed, I mumble these words "Wake Up Girl and PUSH Through!" Even though I'm saying it over and over again. It's only when my feet actually touch the floor that I begin to truly wake up and adjust my *mind* and *attitude*. I'm reminded that it's not about me and how I'm feeling. It's about pleasing God. He wants us to spend time getting to know Him because God is all-knowing and He *already* knows everything about us.

"Wake Up Girl and PUSH Through" is a Choice!! It may be difficult at first, because of thoughts like:

> *"Girl, waking up early in the morning is not important...ANYTIME you spend in the day is good enough because God knows your heart."*

Or maybe thoughts like:

> *"Girl, it's okay if you just push snooze...wake up in another hour or so...it's really not that serious."*

Waking up early to spend time with God must become intentional. Therefore, you must ignore your natural thoughts and emotions, and make a decision that you're going to put God First! By *"Putting God First"* means you spend time with Him before you get dressed... before you get your kids ready for daycare or school... before you prepare breakfast... before you leave out of your house early to avoid morning traffic or to catch a flight...

Designate Morning Alone Time With God

and before you check your social media accounts. Spending time with God is a choice that you make to put Him first before you start your day.

There are so many benefits to gain from waking up early to spend time with God. You just need to be willing to give it a try. Your morning alone time with God should be something you practice doing *"everyday"* so it becomes a habit that happens naturally. *Every day* includes weekdays, weekends, your birthday and even on holidays, you stay committed to still spend time with God. When designating morning alone time with God becomes a habit you will always put Him first. Regardless of what you have planned or how busy your schedule may look, you will "Wake Up Early and PUSH Through" to get your time in with God!

Your morning time with God doesn't have to be the same routine day after day. Ask the Holy Spirit to guide you. There are a variety of meaningful ways to spend quality time with God such as:

1. Praying

2. Reading your bible, but most importantly choose a bible with the translation that you can understand.

3. Writing on index cards some of the scriptures that are referenced in the prayers located in this book. Then practice reading them directly from the card with authority in your voice as you pray and speak directly about your circumstances.

4. Writing in a prayer journal.

5. Studying the names of God that you may not be familiar with that are referenced in the prayers located in this book. Take time to ask the Holy Spirit to lead you to resources that will give you more insight into learning the meaning of God's names, so you can speak them with understanding and boldness.

6. Reading Christian self-help books or devotional materials.

Remember, your goal is to develop a more personal relationship with God and getting to know Him and applying His principles to your life.

Wake Up Girl and PUSH Through!

I believe Prayer should always be included in your time with God. It is by far the *most* essential and powerful tool that you can use to grow and mature spiritually. We all sometimes face difficult circumstances or challenges in our lives, but we should not give up or become discouraged. With every hardship, difficulty and disappointment know that there is *Power in Prayer!*

This book is designed to help you enhance your prayer life while learning to pray effectively with confidence, boldness, and authority. The prayers in this book are Spirit-led, scripture-based, and reference the powerful names and character of God. Begin to use this book as one of your resources and read these prayers aloud with confidence believing that whatever you ask in prayer "In the Name of Jesus" or "In Jesus' Name", believe that you will receive it.

I'm so excited for you and what God is about to do in your life! *Stay encouraged!* When your alarm clock wakes you up early before the sun rises, keep in mind you're not alone... *mine is too*. Remember someone is cheering you on and saying, "Girl, Wake Up and Push Through!"

"We are in this together... So Let's Do It!"

Designate Morning Alone Time With God

01
DEAR GOD,

Being Disciplined and Consistent is what I really struggle with. I always desire to change my habits in my head, but when it's time to put action behind it, I tend to not fully follow through. Jesus, I am asking that You put something "*new*" inside of me. Put something new inside of me that has a sensitivity to your nudge. When I feel in my spirit that I need to wake up early no matter how uncomfortable it may be, help me to "*push*" through!

Jesus, deep down inside I know that I have what it takes to start this new habit. Help me to not focus on the days ahead of me and get overwhelmed before I even try. Help me to put all of my focus into making You my very first priority today and trusting that You will give me the strength I need to be consistent with it on the days ahead of me. I want this to be a Lifestyle change!

A lifestyle change that transforms me into a *new* woman. A woman that I was created and destined to be. I speak right now that the feeling of being lost, incomplete and purposeless will no longer keep me from experiencing life the way You have destined me to experience it.

Jesus, one thing I know is that I cannot do this without You! For years, I have tried and I always quit before I give it a true chance to bring about change in my life, but this time I am declaring that I will not give up. The areas that I know I struggle in the most; I totally surrender them to You. No more excuses for me! I stand on Your Word that says "I can do all things through Christ who strengthens me." (Philippians 4:13) God today is my declaration: I'm All In!

In the name of Jesus that I pray, Amen.

02 DEAR GOD,

Today I'm focusing on taking it one day at a time! You *know* how easily I can overthink things and give up in my mind simply because it *seems* too hard. You *know* how many times I have started spending time with You but give up in my mind simply because it *seems* impossible to *really* do this every single day. I stand firm today, speaking over that negative spirit that tries to attach itself to my mind. In the name of Jesus:

- Never Again will waking up early to spend time with You be hard for me to do because now I am changing my mindset to focus on the "Quality of time" I spend with You and not focusing on the "Quantity of time" I am spending with You.

- Never again will spending time with You feel like a burden. Change my heart, mind, and spirit to get excited to wake up early and start my day in Your presence.

I bind up in the name of Jesus the spirit of doing things just for show… No More! My private time I spend with You will not be broadcasted so I can look like I'm changing to others. I am taking a stand against every attack on my mind and this time…I will "not" be moved!

God, I declare that this time… my actions will speak for itself.

In the name of Jesus that I pray, Amen.

Designate Morning Alone Time With God

DEAR GOD, 03

I ask that You keep me excited for You! As I wake up early, I will not be naive about the fact that this will get hard. I will not go into this thinking that just because I said *"I am going to change my habits"* that it will naturally just come easy to me. No! God, I *know* I need You!

I am like a sheep that needs constant guidance, direction, and correction. You are Jehovah Rohi, which means that You are my Shepherd. Each morning "Guide Me" on what to read in my bible. Each morning "Lead Me" to the resources You want my spirit to be fed with.

- Lead Me, God!
- Guide Me, God!
- You are Jehovah Rohi "My Shepherd"... Yes, You are Jehovah Rohi "My Shepherd"!

Every move I make from this day forward will be led by Your Holy Spirit. As the Holy Spirit guides me, help me to be sensitive to it and forgive me in advance for any kind of kickback I may give unknowingly by not fully being obedient.

Thank You Jesus for what You are doing on the inside of me! Transform me from the *inside*... Out!

In the name of Jesus that I pray, Amen.

04 DEAR GOD,

Thank You for changing my thoughts and perceptions of You! Since I have chosen to "*Wake Up Early*", my mindset has shifted to being all about You being "*first*" in my life. Your Word says "But seek first the kingdom of God and His righteousness, and all these things shall be added to you." (Matthew 6:33) So, today I Thank You for not allowing me to get up and get moving *before* I spend quality time with You.

Help me to remain steadfast in seeking Your Face and not just Your Hand! Seeking Your face is learning and growing deeper in the knowledge of You and truly falling in love with You, just simply for "*Who You are!*"

Change my ways when I try to hide and not give You my all with my efforts. I declare today that I will not half-step! With every moment, I want to keep my spirit close and connected to You. As I stay close to You, Favor will be released to me!

Yes, In the name of Jesus, I decree and I declare that the favor of God is being released to me right now as I speak!

Jesus, Help me to remain obedient with putting You *first* because I know that if I continue to Push Through and do just that... being favored and blessings *absolutely* come with the territory! So, I ask in the name of Jesus that You help me not to hinder my blessings not a second longer because of my delayed obedience, keep me close to You as I try...because God, You know that... I truly am trying!

In Jesus' name, Amen.

Designate Morning Alone Time With God

DEAR GOD, 05

I ask that You work on the inside of me so that everything I *say, think and do* is with a pure heart that is pleasing in Your sight! Every morning that I "*Push Through*" and spend time with You… it is preparing me for what You have already in store for me.

So today, I am standing in expectancy knowing that You will surprise me with never seen before favor, guidance, and wisdom. Every step I make will be favored and every room I walk in, favor will follow me. Why? Because Your Word says, " For I know the plans I have for you," declares the LORD, "plans to prosper you and not to harm you, plans to give you hope and a future." (Jeremiah 29:11)

So as I move about my day, God, I ask that You open up doors for me, make opportunities available to me and send in people that will be a blessing to me. When I walk through the doors, as I say yes to the opportunities and as I interact with people…I ask that You keep me focused on acknowledging You so that You are the *only* one that gets the glory!

Oh! You know the plans You have for me, so today I ask that You help me to scratch my plans and go with Your flow! As I follow Your lead for my life… I will prosper in everything I put my mind to.

Thank You Jesus, in advance for how You are going to completely blow my mind! I am standing in expectancy for it and with boldness. I declare that my Faith calls it *Done*!

In the name of Jesus that I pray, Amen.

SPIRITUAL GROWTH IS A MARATHON, NOT A SPRINT!

Designate Morning Alone Time With God

06
DEAR GOD,

I know that it is because I am spending time with You early in the morning that I have been feeling renewed in every area of my life. God, I know that it is because I decided to put You *first* before doing anything else that my mind and heart feel restored. I thank You for being Elohim, which means that You are the Creator and my Restorer. Yes, God! I feel it happening on the inside and I know that it's *All You*! I ask that You help me to keep *Pushing Through* with Your strength fueling me day after day!

No matter what I face today, no matter what I have on my agenda to do, No matter how busy my schedule is… Keep me Focused!

Every day continue to restore my spirit so that Anxiety from the issues of my life will not overtake me! Thank You for being Jehovah Shalom, which means "You are my Peace!" My Peace that takes away Anxiety, My Peace that takes away Depression, My Peace that takes away Fear, Yes, God, My Peace that takes away Doubt! *You…are… Jehovah Shalom, My Peace!*

So I ask in the name of Jesus that You keep restoring my heart, mind, body, and spirit. Give me the kind of peace that *cannot* be shaken or stirred up. Give me the peace of God that surpasses all understanding!

In Jesus' name, Amen.

07 DEAR GOD,

As I wake up to spend time with You, help me not to just go through the motion, but help me to make it count. As I create routines that turn into habits, help me not to just be satisfied with an *attempt*... but help me to be spiritually mature enough to give it my *All*.

I ask in the name of Jesus that You:

- Show me how to truly worship and be confident in knowing that the words from my mouth are powerful and are like music to Your ears.

- Show me how to pray on my face in a *position* of surrender that shows true humility for Your character and nature, even if it feels weird, awkward and uncomfortable.

- Show me how to read my Bible for truth and understanding and be fully obedient to the Holy Spirit when He guides me to biblical resources for the parts that I can't fully grasp.

Yes, God! I am giving it my All and making every moment I spend with You count! Thank You Jesus, for my growth because I know that spiritual maturity is a marathon and not a sprint!

I decree and I declare in the name of Jesus, today I *will not* leave Your presence without feeling Your spirit revitalize me. I am maturing and growing and My God, It feels so good!

In the name of Jesus that I pray, Amen.

Designate Morning Alone Time With God

DEAR GOD, 08

Thank You for the flow in my morning routine that You are helping me to create! Honestly, sometimes I wake up and have no idea what I am going to read or pray about, but each time the Holy Spirit sends something that speaks directly to me and my situation and I know that each time that was *You* moving!

Each time I know that the confirming words I read or hear... is Your way of *speaking* to me so that *You* can get my attention. Jesus, I ask that You send biblical resources my way! Everything that I am confused about, I ask that You give me clarity and wisdom. What I don't understand, help me not to get frustrated or overwhelmed...but instead lead me in the right direction to research and find tools that are practical and easy to comprehend.

- I refuse to allow the enemy to make me feel like I will never grow spiritually.
- I refuse to allow the enemy to make me feel like everything is too advanced for me.
- I refuse to allow the enemy to make me feel like me trying is going nowhere.

The devil is a *lie* and every day that I "Push Through"... I am proving the enemy absolutely *wrong*! Thank You Jesus, for the boldness You are giving me against the devil and his tactics against my mind. Devil, in the name of Jesus, I serve you notice that today "It stops here!"

In the name of Jesus that I pray, Amen.

09 DEAR GOD,

"I can do all things through Christ who strengthens me" (Philippians 4:13) that's what Your Word says. So, even when I get frustrated and feel like I need help getting into the groove of being disciplined and consistent.

I will keep Your Word flowing through my mouth over and over and over:

- When it's hard for me to wake up early in the morning..."I can do all things through Christ who strengthens me!"

- When I'm reading my Bible and I get immediately bored or overwhelmed..."I can do all things through Christ who strengthens me!"

- When I'm writing in my prayer journal and I feel like everything I write is so scripted and it's not really me being open and honest about how I truly feel about my life and I just want to stop altogether... "I can do all things through Christ who strengthens me!"

I decree and I declare in the name of Jesus Self- Discipline and Consistency will *not* be hard for me! Jesus, You are working on the inside of me strengthening every weak area in my mind. I speak that day by day I will become stronger and stronger in You.

God, I am so proud of myself thus far and I ask that You keep Obedience being my driving force.

In the name of Jesus that I pray, Amen.

Designate Morning Alone Time With God

DEAR GOD, 10

I know that You see all and You know all! So, why does it feel like every morning I have to constantly fight for my peace! If it's not from outside worries and burdens weighing me down, then it's from the thoughts and opinions of other people getting inside my head. Jesus, help me not to be easily stressed and bothered by things that I do not have control over. Show me how to relinquish them to You because the battle is not mine it is Yours!

That's it! The battle is not mine, *it is Yours*, I have to remember that when distractions try to ruin my time that I spend with You in the morning.

God, right now I call on Your name which is Jehovah Tsaba! Jehovah Tsaba, which means "You are my Warrior!" In this spiritual battle that I deal with, You are working it all out for me because You are an army all by Yourself! I don't have to feel like I am alone and that I have to handle things that attack me on my own. I have confidence knowing that I can call on Your name and by Faith, the atmosphere immediately *shifts*!

This morning, I decree and I declare in the name of Jesus that I will never again waste another second of my energy or time focusing on the distractions that try to interrupt my focus being on You. Instead, I will *Push Through* despite it all, because I know I have someone *greater* fighting my battles for me! That someone is Jehovah Tsaba, *My Warrior... My Warrior... My-- Warrior!*

In the name of Jesus that I pray, Amen.

I CHOOSE TO MAKE MY TIME WITH GOD COUNT!

Designate Morning Alone Time With God

DEAR GOD, 11

Thank You for how You are filling me up in the morning when I spend time with You. It's like...You know exactly what I need even before I know I need it and that's because You are Omniscient which is *"All-Knowing"* and I love how you already know what I need even before I get a chance to tell You.

So, when I start reading my bible, You always tend to send confirming words that reassure me that You are moving on my behalf! *I love that!*

Today, I humbly ask that You continue to change my mindset, shift my thinking and expand my spiritual perspective. You are Omnipotent which is *"All-Powerful"* and You have all the power to turn every negative situation around for my good.

Jesus, Thank You! Thank You! Thank You!

I feel Your Presence not just in the morning but all throughout my day!

I'm so grateful to be close to You!

In the name of Jesus that I pray, Amen.

12 DEAR GOD,

This what I am doing which is spending quality time with You every morning before doing anything else... is not a small thing! No Sir! "*This*" is major, "*This*" is where the shift takes place, "*This*" is where the overflow comes from and *This* is where I stand firmly on Your Word that says "But as it is written, Eye has not seen, nor ear heard, Nor have entered into the heart of man, The things which God has prepared for those who love Him." (1 Corinthians 2:9) So, I confess today that I love You! I confess today that I need You! I confess today that I want *You* and *only You*!

At this moment, Jesus I want to say Thank You in advance for every blessing that is in transit with *my name on it*:

- My Husband that is pre-ordained by You has *my name on it*, I stand on Your Word and by Faith; I call it forth in the name of Jesus!

- My healthy pregnancy with safe labor and delivery has *my name on it*, I stand on Your Word and by Faith; I call it forth in the name of Jesus.

- Bonuses, promotions, and increase in my job and my business has *my name on it*, I stand on Your Word and by Faith; I call it forth in the name of Jesus!

- Leaving a legacy for my children's children has *my name on it*, I stand on Your Word and by Faith; I call it forth in the name of Jesus.

I thank You in advance for how You are going to blow my mind! Just envisioning it brings a real smile to my face! I love You God and I mean that with everything in me!

In the name of Jesus that I pray, Amen.

Designate Morning Alone Time With God

DEAR GOD, 13

Never again will I make an excuse *not* to obey You! As I am growing spiritually, I ask that You allow the Holy Spirit to tug at me, pull on me, make me uncomfortable, and interrupt my sleep until I choose to say "Yes God, I will obey You", *even* when I do not fully understand what it is that You are telling me to do.

God, I trust that You will confirm every part where I am uncertain. The more I spend time with You, the easier it will become for me to *hear* Your voice leading me and guiding me.

Your Word says, "And let us not be weary in well doing: for in due season we shall reap, if we faint not."(Galatians 6:9) So, Jesus, I ask that You help me not to grow weary or get frustrated if it seems like I am not seeing You move. Show me how to "*Be Still*" and declutter my heart and mind so that I can get into the position of Surrender to clearly hear from You and learn a lesson in Patience. In my position of surrender on my knees and on my face, I open my heart to You!

Lord, I know I have been using the word obedient a lot lately, but that's because I'm completely *all in* and *this* is the area that I really need help with because even when I *think* I am doing right, I need You to confirm it each and every time. I know there is a season for everything, so I ask that You help me to be diligent and patient because I trust that "My Time is Coming Up Next!"

In Jesus' name, Amen.

14 DEAR GOD,

Thank You for *who* You are and *what* You mean to me! I will forever glorify Your name! As I am waking up early to spend time with You, I will start *speaking* over my life like never before! I stand on Your word that says "Death and life are in the power of the tongue, And those who love it will eat its fruit." (Proverbs 18:21)... so today I speak life and life more abundantly!

- I speak protection over my life, in the name of Jesus, from every hidden assignment of the enemy that tries to steal, kill and destroy my future.

- I speak healing over my life, in the name of Jesus, and I bind up every sickness and disease that disguises itself as a hereditary trait passed down by genetics.

- I speak abundance over my life, in the name of Jesus, and I bind up every poverty-stricken mentality of lack and struggle.

No longer will I be timid or lack confidence when I am speaking over my life because when I speak Your name *"Jesus",* Power exudes through me because I have You living on the inside of me. Fear you *cannot* live here, *You Must Go!* Low self-esteem, you *cannot* live here, *You Must Go!* I am a powerful woman of God and my boldness is not one to be messed with.

Devil, in the name of Jesus I serve you notice right now, that I am coming for everything you stole from me! God has my back and I am no longer Weak and vulnerable to your tactics. My life is covered by the Blood of Jesus and I have authority over you. From this day forward, just watch how I move with *no* Fear!

In Jesus' name, Amen.

Designate Morning Alone Time With God

DEAR GOD, 15

I will stand strong in You today! Every morning that I wake up to designate morning alone time with You is making me mentally, emotionally and spiritually stronger than I ever could imagine. I'm stronger in my mind, I'm stronger in my heart and I'm stronger in my spirit… I will *not* bend, I will *not* break and I will *not* fall!

I will stand firm in God's Word knowing that when I *speak* mountains move and a supernatural *shift* happens because there is *power* in the tongue:

- I *speak* in the name of Jesus that there is *no* lack in my life because You are El Shaddai, which means that "You are God Almighty." You are more than enough! I have an infinite supply of what I need because You are powerful enough to provide it!

- I *speak* in the name of Jesus that I am the head and I'm not the tail, that I am above and I'm not beneath. Jehovah Jireh, "You are My Provider" and I want for *nothing!*

- I *speak* in the name of Jesus that begging and borrowing is a thing of the *past*. I am a lender and I'm *not* a borrower, the windows of heaven will pour me out a blessing that I will not have room enough to receive!

God, I know that *this* kind of language is *powerful* so, *I Speak It…I Speak It…I Speak It…* and my Faith calls it *Done*!

In the name of Jesus that I pray, Amen.

THOSE CONNECTED TO ME ARE BLESSED!

Designate Morning Alone Time With God

DEAR GOD, 16

I love You for being Omni-benevolent, which means that "You are Infinitely Good." You are so good to me and I want to ask for forgiveness for each time my thoughts are not solely on You early in the morning.

Sometimes it seems like my mind is filled with what I need, what I want and what I'm trying to do that it becomes foggy and I barely can focus on reading my bible or praying.

Help me, Jesus! Help my morning time with You, not to be cluttered because of my plans and my agenda. God, I ask in the name of Jesus that *You* completely scratch my plans and allow me to go with Your flow!

I stand on Your word that says "Be anxious for nothing, but in everything by prayer and supplication, with thanksgiving, let your requests be made known to God; and the peace of God, which surpasses all understanding, will guard your hearts and minds through Christ Jesus."

(Philippians 4:6-7)

So, today I ask that You clear my thoughts! As I spend time with You, help me to have tunnel vision and stay *focused*. God, today I decree and I declare that from this moment forward *everything will wait* because I'm *serious* about putting *You* first!

In the name of Jesus that I pray, Amen.

17 DEAR GOD,

You are absolutely amazing beyond my imagination and I just want to Thank You for not giving up on me, when I *wanted* to give up on myself. Today, I ask that You allow me to take the time to *enjoy* the life You have given to me. I ask that You help me to *enjoy* the simple things that money can't buy!

As I enjoy life just as it is now, I ask that You help me to bring love, hope, and joy into someone else's life!

My morning time with You always puts me in a great mood, so I ask that You make it possible for me to make at least *one* person smile, feel special and feel loved... all because "*You are love.*"

Today, I am making it my mission to spread Joy in some way, shape or form so that when people *see me*...they *see* Christ in me!

Jesus, I ask that You take away the nervousness to speak Your name in front of others. Help me not be afraid to let others know that I believe in You! Help my spirit that is filled with Your love to speak *for* me in everything I do and say. I ask that You help my fruit to be seen and people know that I am Your child. I know You are working on me Lord, and I ask that You help me to be a good representation of You!

In Jesus' name, Amen.

Designate Morning Alone Time With God

DEAR GOD, 18

Thank You for this second, this minute and this hour! Thank you for my sound mind that allows me to make good choices. I chose to start a habit of spending time with You in the morning and I love how I'm feeling renewed and totally revitalized from it!

Jesus, help me to do a self-check and dig deep to find *any* area that is so deeply rooted that it has remained untouched by *You*! You are Omniscient which is "All-knowing" and You already know how I think and I can't change, develop, grow or mature alone!

I need You to walk with me, talk with me and guide me on *how* to open up fully to You so that *every* part of my life will be restored by *You*!

From this day forward, I want to walk the walk and talk the talk and I only can do that by *not* leaving any room for the enemy to attack and use against me. I come to you right now declaring that I am fully surrendered to You!

Thank You in advance for what You are already doing and for what You are going to do in every dimension of my life!

In Jesus' name, Amen.

19 DEAR GOD,

I am careful to reverence You in everything because *with* You *nothing* is impossible! You are Omnipotent, which is "All-Powerful" and You deserve to get the praise, honor, and glory! I thank You for Your Word that says "You will keep in perfect peace, those whose minds are steadfast because they trust in You." (Isaiah 26:3) So daily, I will wait and Trust You to direct my path because through *your* direction comes my complete *blessing*!

The way I feel right now after spending time with You makes me *never again* walk in doubt or fear about what You have coming for me! I have perfect peace not because everything is worked out, but because I have *You* working on my behalf!

- Every connection and opportunity that I want to come my way *will happen* because You will *bless* me with it.

- The career that I truly want *is coming* because *You* will *bless* me with it!

- The loving, loyal and committed husband that I want *is coming* because *You* will *bless* me with it!

Devil, in the name of Jesus I come to you right now binding up *every* negative thought that tries to make me feel like it is *too late* for me to get the desires of my heart! You are a lie! I stand in expectancy of a multitude of *blessings* coming my way! I speak blessings that exceed my expectations and truly blow my mind!

In the name of Jesus that I pray, Amen.

Designate Morning Alone Time With God

DEAR GOD, 20

Something has *shifted* in my life and it feels *so* good! Thank You for what You have been doing *in and through* me ever since I started pushing myself to wake up early and spend quality time with You.

Lately, I use wisdom when I make decisions and I am slow to anger and easy to show love and compassion. Jesus, I am *not* the same and it's all because of You.

Today, I ask that You help others to recognize what You have done on the inside of me by how I *move, talk* and *react* differently. I want them to feel my spirit and energy and know that there is something different about me.

Jesus, *this* feeling is what I have been missing in my life and once I stopped trying to be in control, You have allowed my mornings just to *flow* in your spirit. I absolutely love it!

God, I glorify Your name because I am growing and evolving into the woman that You destined me to be! Slowly but surely, I will continue to make You proud by consistently keeping my focus on You. I seriously love You and every morning I will continue to prove it to You!

In the name of Jesus that I pray, Amen.

MY ACTIONS SPEAK VOLUMES FOR ITSELF...

Designate Morning Alone Time With God

DEAR GOD, 21

I *love* how You strengthened and equipped me to do things that I never imagined I would truly be able to do! You are my *strength*! My mornings are forever changed because *now* I am hooked on "Waking Up and Pushing Through!"

Thank You for "*this*" spiritual *breakthrough*!

- Every day I am learning more and more about Your character and Your Nature.
- Every day I am growing and developing into a person that Christ shines through!

When I walk through a door my light shines bright, my energy and spirit shift the atmosphere and my entire presence is saturated with Christ exuding through *me*! Thank You, Jesus!

I decree and I declare in the name of Jesus that "designating morning alone time with You" is every day for me now... and God, I'm *never* going back!

In Jesus' name, Amen.

22 DEAR GOD,

Sometimes when I pray, read or write in my prayer journal my thoughts begin to drift and I start to think about all the things that I'm dealing with or have to handle. I know that *"this"* is nothing but an attack on my mind so that I will *give up* on spending time with You.

Jesus, help me to *recognize* when the enemy is trying to sneak in to interrupt my morning time with You. I have Authority over the enemy, and God Your word says, "Whatever you bind on earth will be bound in heaven, and whatever you loose on earth will be loosed in heaven" (Matthew 18:18)

So right now in the name of Jesus…

- I *bind up* worry and I *loose* the peace of God that surpasses all understanding about the issues I face in my home, in my finances, and on my job.

- I *bind up* lack and I *loose* a complete abundance of overflow in my financial well-being, where I am no longer living check-to-check, but I am blessed to be a blessing.

- I *bind up* sickness and I *loose* Your healing power over depression, anxiety, bipolar' ism and any other trait of a generational curse that tries to attach itself to my mind and body.

God, I thank You for the *shift* that You are creating in my mind right now! I thank You for the confidence I have to speak to the enemy and command him to take his hands off my thoughts and my mind.

In the name of Jesus that I pray, Amen.

Designate Morning Alone Time With God

DEAR GOD, 23

Since I have been designating morning alone time with You, I seriously feel like I can do anything! Everything that I am putting my mind to seems to just *flow* and I know that's *all* because of *You*.

The things that normally would have me nervous about trying or stepping into, I now take small action steps of Faith with boldness and confidence.

- I'm excited about what is to come in my life!
- I'm excited to watch how favor chases me down in everything that I do!
- I'm excited to watch how overflow begins to pour into my lap, that's pressed down, shaken together and running over!

But Father God, I ask that as the excitement continues to rise daily from the expectancy of Your blessings, help me to remain *patient* for it! Your Word says, "Be anxious for nothing, but in everything by prayer and supplication, with thanksgiving, let your requests be made known to God; and the peace of God, which surpasses all understanding, will guard your hearts and minds through Christ Jesus." (Philippians 4:6-7)

So, I am grateful that my excitement is here *but* I will make sure that I focus not on just receiving the blessing but remembering that Obedience brings the blessing.

In the name of Jesus that I pray, Amen.

24 DEAR GOD,

It feels *so* good to feel seen by You!

It's like with me making this *one* decision daily to *"Push Through"* and designate morning alone time with You, You are opening my eyes to recognize that *this* was the secret to unlocking a new dimension of my life.

"*This* feels good…*I* feel good… and *Life* is good!" Even while things are not perfect and I need help with so much, I still feel amazing deep down inside because my hope is in *You*!

My hope about my relationship, my home, my family, my job and my finances all have changed from *"I don't know how this is going to happen"* -to- " *I can't wait to see how God does this."*

Thank You Jesus, for changing my attitude, perspective and approach about every part of my life. I now view myself, my situation and other people in a positive way and I know that it's *only* because of my personal relationship with You that I am able to do so.

Jesus, I ask that You keep me close to You so that I can feel like *this* all of the time!

In the name of Jesus that I pray, Amen.

Designate Morning Alone Time With God

DEAR GOD, 25

If I can be honest with You for a minute, some days I feel like I'm losing hope! It seems like everything I am trying to do is failing even when I know I have the right intentions behind it. Show me what I am doing so wrong?

Jesus, I humbly come to You right now asking that You *open* my eyes to see what *You* see. Show me parts of myself and my life that I have blinders on about. Reveal what's deep down inside of me that I am too afraid to fully surrender to You...

- If it's a habit I need to break, Holy Spirit convict me and make God's voice clear to me and *show* me how to change it one day at a time.
- If it's someone that I need to forgive, *show* me how to reach out to them and humbly ask for forgiveness *even* if I don't feel like I am the wrong one.

Make it clear to me as I spend quality time with You what it is I need to *do* to walk in *complete* obedience. From this day forward, I will not question myself about what I am doing so *wrong*...instead, I will put all my focus on what I *know is right* and that is completely and wholeheartedly trusting You.

Today, I decree and I declare in the name of Jesus I will *not* hinder my blessings any longer due to delayed obedience. I am making the change and sticking to it.

In the name of Jesus that I pray, Amen.

MY SPIRITUAL FOUNDATION IS GROWING!

Designate Morning Alone Time With God

DEAR GOD, 26

Somedays I wake up early to spend time with You and all I seem to pray about is what I need *help* with.

I want to learn how to pray and speak Your name with boldness and confidence. I want to learn how to pray and speak *life* into my spirit by Your character. So, today I speak that:

- You are Alpha and Omega (The Beginning and The End)... *Yes, God, That's Who You Are!*
- You are Jehovah Jireh (My Provider), Jehovah Shalom (My Peace), Jehovah Rapha (My Healer), Jehovah Rohi (My Shepherd), Jehovah Nissi (My Banner in a Spiritual Battle) and Jehovah Tsaba (My Warrior)... *Yes, God, That's Who You Are!*
- You are Omniscient (All-Knowing), Omnipotent (All-Powerful), Omnipresent (All-Present) and Omnibenevolent (Infinitely Good)... *Yes, God, That's Who You Are!*

Right now, there's a *fire* inside of me that desires to pray with authority. Every day, that I spend time with You in the morning I will practice speaking *"Who You Are"* out loud so that it becomes comfortable in my spirit, and the more and more I do it, the more confident I will become and the words will naturally just flow!

In the name of Jesus that I pray, Amen.

27 DEAR GOD,

"An Overflow of Blessings are on the Way!" and I thank You in advance for it!

Your Word says "Give, and it will be given to you. A good measure, pressed down, shaken together and running over, will be poured into your lap. For with the measure you use, it will be measured to you." (Luke 6:38)

So, this morning as I spend time with You, I praise You in advance for the Super-natural *Overflow*! Receiving overflow will allow me to be a blessing to others where I am not selfishly only thinking of myself but having the heart to be like Christ and serve. Serving others allows me to pour into them and give without my hand being out to receive!

Thank You, for me being the example of what a woman of God looks like strictly by *what I do* and *how I treat people.*

God, pour out a blessing that I don't have room enough to receive so that I can pour into someone else's life too.

In the name of Jesus that I pray, Amen.

Designate Morning Alone Time With God

DEAR GOD, 28

I woke up this morning with boldness inside of me to speak over my life! Through the time that I spend with You, it's really helping me boost my self-esteem and gives me the confidence to know that I can do *anything* I truly set my heart out to do!

No matter how hard it is sometimes... I'm so grateful for Your strength because I'm *doing* it and I'm *so* proud of myself! God, doing *this* lets me know that I have what it takes in other areas of my life as well if I continue to *put You first* before everything!

So today:

- I speak over my life and I ask that You show me my purpose! Show me how to take every setback, heartache, disappointment, failure, and pain and turn it around to glorify Your name.

- I speak over my life and I decree and I declare that my *story* will be my *testimony*! No more fear, no more shame, and no more doubt! Even through nervousness, I will trust that the Holy Spirit will give me the vision to birth whatever You put inside of me. Equip me to be able to execute it not for my personal gain but to be used by Christ and let my light shine.

God, they will see that because *You* did it for me...*You will* do it for them too! Use me, God, for Your Glory... more than ever before I'm *Ready*!

In the name of Jesus that I pray, Amen.

29 DEAR GOD,

I love how your Word is starting to make sense to me now! I mean it is really hitting my core and I can see how throughout the day I remember things that I read from my morning time with You and some part of it helps me get through situations I face.

That's nobody but You that is allowing everything I do to become full-circle and connect with each other to *keep* me in Your presence.

Where I once was quick-tempered and eager to speak my mind *now* I am slow-to-speak and slow-to-anger, which is something like a *miracle* for me!

God, You know me better than anyone else, so I ask that You keep me grounded in You. Your word says, "You will keep in perfect peace those whose minds are steadfast because they trust in You." (Isaiah 26:3)

So, I ask that You continue to work on my heart and keep it pure for You because I truly do trust You! Day-by-day keep me in *Your* perfect peace.

In Jesus' name, Amen.

Designate Morning Alone Time With God

DEAR GOD, 30

No Matter What! I will keep pushing and keep trying! For everything that I felt was a setback, was nothing but a setup for You to get the glory.

The yes, the no and the not yet I have ever been told in my life all are making sense to me now!

I stand on Your word that says, "God *is* not a man, that He should lie, Nor a son of man, that He should repent. Has He said, and will He not do? Or has He spoken, and will He not make it good?" (Numbers 23:19)

This scripture *fires* me up! I love it when it says, *"God is not a man that He should lie!"*, That *one* statement confirms that *"You will always be Who You have always been"* and just like You were with the many people I read about in my bible, *so You are with me Now!*

So the more I read my bible in the morning, the more I grow with understanding to be able to stand on every word that tells me Your promises for me.

Every promise in Your word will manifest in my life and knowing that gives me Strength! God, You are faithful!

In Jesus' name, Amen.

MY PRAYER LIFE IS MY SECRET WEAPON!

Designate Morning Alone Time With God

DEAR GOD, 31

Who would've known that waking up early to designate morning alone time with You would be what restores my inner core? *It has!* This one change in my habits has revitalized my view on life as a whole. And Man! It feels so good!

God, You know how sometimes…just out of nowhere… I would start to feel so out of it and couldn't necessarily put my finger on what was really bothering me. That whole feeling has changed and I have to say "Thank You, Jesus!"

Since, I have been reading my bible, praying, writing, and truly worshiping You in my private time, I seriously do not feel like that anymore! Yes, things still bother me but I *handle* them *so* much better now! Only You made that possible!

I'm so grateful for You being Elohim, which means that "You are My Creator and my Restorer!" You have restored my mind to "go-after" You and "seek" You with a receptive spirit and open heart!

Holy Spirit give me Godly wisdom in every situation I face and with every move I make because, God, I am truly *all in* for You!

In the name of Jesus that I pray, Amen.

32 DEAR GOD,

Instead of complaining and being in "worry mode" about what is going on in my life, I'm saying *"God, I Trust You!"*

I know that this is *all* a test of my Faith! But, not only just a test of my faith but also my willingness to *completely* Trust You and not just by me *saying* it but fully *believing* it in my heart.

Even when things are falling apart right before my eyes, God, I know it's like You're saying, "Yes, I see what's going on…But will you trust Me?"

So today, I am boldly stating… "YES! I Trust You, God!"

- With bills coming from the left and the right… and every month it seems to get harder and harder to pay them on time… *I Still Trust You!* Why? Because You are Jehovah Jireh, My Provider and Your Word says, "My God shall supply all your need according to His riches in glory by Christ Jesus." (Philippians 4:19) Yes! *That's why I Trust You!*

- With my home in shambles from attitudes and arguments that seem to keep being fueled over the smallest things… *I Still Trust You!* Why? Because You are Jehovah Nissi, My Banner that I wave in a Spiritual Battle and *Yes! That's why I Trust You!*

No matter what I face or what comes my way, I will continue to stand firm in my commitment to Trust You!

In the name of Jesus that I pray, Amen.

Designate Morning Alone Time With God

DEAR GOD, 33

The Holy Spirit is so powerful! Before I started designating morning alone time with You… I never fully understood *"Who"* the Holy Spirit is, *"What"* the Holy Spirit does and *"How"* the Holy Spirit works.

Oh!! *But now,* I totally understand how He works because *every* morning that I *Push Through*….I'm getting a first-hand experience of the Holy Spirit at work on my behalf.

- I recognize *now* that it's only through the *help* of the Holy Spirit that I can read my bible and dig deep to understand the people in it and their stories. *But not only that, but* then take it up a notch by giving me spiritual wisdom to be able to relate it to my own personal life. *That's the Holy Spirit!*

- I recognize *now* that it's only through the *help* of the Holy Spirit that equips me to read & learn scriptures. *But not only that, but* then take it up a notch and be able to apply them to my life with boldness and authority. *That's the Holy Spirit!*

That's *all* the Holy Spirit! So, today I say Thank You Jesus for sending me *real* help. Continue to send biblical resources like books and sermons that can teach me more about the Holy Spirit and how I can practice recognizing His whispers, to be obedient to His nudges.

In the name of Jesus that I pray, Amen.

34 DEAR GOD,

Each morning I feel myself gaining confidence in my prayer life. I feel my personal relationship with You growing stronger and stronger and it's all because of me changing my habits to make spending time with You *"priority!"*

It seems like that was the missing piece to my spiritual growth and I love how now I feel the *power* coming through my voice when I say the name of *Jesus!* That's nobody but You because for some reason I used to be so timid when it came to saying "Jesus Christ" out loud.

No More doubt or nervousness! Today, as I pray… I say *Jesus* with confidence! Oh! Yes! As I worship… I say *Jesus* with boldness!

- JESUS!
- JESUS!
- JESUS!
- I lift up Your majestic name, JESUS!
- JESUS!
- JESUS!
- JESUS!
- I magnify Your Holy name, JESUS!

Thank You, God, for taking my prayer life to the next level! I feel absolutely unstoppable!

In the name of Jesus that I pray, Amen.

Designate Morning Alone Time With God

DEAR GOD, 35

My mornings are forever changed since I spend *each* one with You! I love how designating morning alone time with You was my very own decision that nobody had to *force* me to do. Every day I wake up with an open heart for the Holy Spirit to have His way!

That's what I call Spiritual Maturity! I know that Spiritual Maturity doesn't come with age, but it comes from a change of habits.

Thank You Jesus for Your transforming power! I seriously feel You "changing"me and it's because of *You* that I feel like a whole new being! I no longer hesitate or overthink what I'm doing but instead, I allow it to just *flow*!

God, I know You see me trying! So today, I ask In the name of Jesus that You keep my thoughts and actions sensitive to your constant nudges and continue to grow me spiritually to be the best Me I possibly can be.

In the name of Jesus that I pray, Amen.

GOD IS THE SOURCE OF MY BLESSINGS!

Designate Morning Alone Time With God

DEAR GOD, 36

Oh! The way You have been blessing me these past few days, I know could only come from You! It's like the blessings keep coming in every direction and I know it's Nobody But You, God!

I love how Your word says "Jesus replied, "What is impossible with man is possible with God." (Luke 18:27) So, I stand on that scripture being my life as living proof because what You have done for me was viewed as *impossible* to the natural eye. Every odd that was against me, *still* couldn't stop the blessing You had for me. You did it for me! I seriously cannot say "Thank You" enough!

Thank You Jesus! Thank You Jesus! Thank You Jesus!

As I receive an overflow of blessings Father, I ask that You keep my heart humble and my motives pure so that I can prove to You that I can be a good steward over what You have given me! I ask that You check my heart and motives behind every single thing I do so that people consistently see Christ through me.

Lord, as humble as I can be, I want to say that "If You don't bless me with anything else ever in life, I am truly grateful for You loving me the way you do even when I don't deserve it and granting me the desires of my heart."

In Jesus' name, Amen.

37 DEAR GOD,

Thank You for birthing a *"New Me"*, who is disciplined and consistent in making a change in my habits. The habit that I am forming of spending time with You early in the morning is shedding light on other areas of my life that I need You to take control of.

God, I no longer want to be afraid to step-out on Faith and go after my dreams! No matter how far behind I think I may be…I know that everything I have done to this point was to prepare me for what You have destined me to become. The rejections, the failed plans and the disappointments were all to get me *here!*

So as I spend time in Your presence this morning, help me to remember and internalize Your Word that says "And we know that all things work together for good to those who love God, to those who are the called according to *His* purpose." (Romans 8:28)

I no longer want to use my past as a reason why I didn't pursue my dreams, but instead, I want to use my past as a way to bring out my story and share my testimony of *where I have been*, *where I could be* and *where God is taking me*! People need to see why I don't look like what I have been through and that's because of *You*! Thank You for finding the lost parts of me and bringing them back to Life! Nothing about my past mistakes can hold me back from what You are doing on the inside of me!

God, I humble myself before You and ask that You help someone else be a better person because I shared my story of what You did for me!

In the name of Jesus that I pray, Amen.

Designate Morning Alone Time With God

DEAR GOD, 38

Help me to keep my momentum going! I have been waking up early and *Pushing Through* and I feel so good afterward!

But Jesus, one thing I don't want to do is become complacent with just the *action*. The action of just waking up and going through the motion but not feeling Your glory move through me that ignites my soul!

Jesus, Help me to be on *Fire* every morning! Give me a supernatural boost of energy so as I sit in my quiet place, I feel Your presence all around me! Your word says, "And whatever you ask in My name, that I will do, that the Father may be glorified in the Son." (John 14:13)

So God:

- I ask in the name of Jesus that You keep me pumped up for You so that when others see me in the afternoon and at night they see the residue of the overflow of anointing and power I had from the morning.

- I ask in the name of Jesus that You help me to open up my heart towards You so that every morning I learn something new about Your character that in turn transforms my very own character where I have integrity in everything I do.

I am being Obedient, Disciplined and Consistent to change my habits and I am proud to say that I have been staying *focused*! Keep me Focused and keep me going! Every morning I'm running after You God because with me having You, I have everything I need.

In Jesus' name, Amen.

39 DEAR GOD,

I have been through so much and I feel so lost and incomplete. It's like every day I'm trying to figure out how the pieces of my life all connect.

God, You know me! You know the deep dark pain and hurt that I keep to myself and try so hard to cover up with a smile. This morning as I spend time with You I ask that You show me how to not allow my past to keep me in bondage mentally, emotionally, and spiritually. Your word says, "For I know the plans I have for you," declares the Lord, "plans to prosper you and not to harm you, plans to give you hope and a future." (Jeremiah 29:11) I trust Your Word God!

So with power and authority that believing in Jesus Christ grants me:

- I decree and I declare in the name of Jesus that my past trauma will no longer keep me embarrassed, afraid or ashamed. Instead, I will walk in God's love to those who hurt me and boldly use my voice to share my story of strength and triumph.

- I decree and I declare in the name of Jesus that the depression, suicidal thoughts, and shame *stops with me* and will "*not*" pass down to my children by disguising itself in any other form for generations to come!

This generational curse stops here! Devil, in Jesus' name you have no power and I command you to take your hands off me and my family and at this very moment, my Faith calls it *Done*!

In the name of Jesus that I pray, Amen.

Designate Morning Alone Time With God

DEAR GOD, 40

Lately, I have been waking up filled to the max with ideas, thoughts, and visions running through my mind where it feels like something is on the inside that needs to be birthed!

Every morning that I spend with You, I feel Your presence confirming all of these visions and it's like a blueprint is being mapped out in front of me. Holy Spirit I need You! I need You to show me how to execute everything You are putting inside of me. It's been so heavy on my mind and spirit that I know it is going to be *big* and surely make the enemy upset.

So I speak over my life and my purpose that You are showing me and...

- I bind in the name of Jesus any hidden motives of my mind and heart that only think about financial gain instead of focusing on how You can get glorified in it.
- I bind in the name of Jesus selfish behavior and a deceptive spirit that wants to take the quick route instead of trusting Your perfect timing!
- I bind in the name of Jesus prideful thoughts that will make me look down on others instead of finding a way to be a surprise blessing that lifts them up.

God, whatever You are pouring in and pulling out of me, bless it so that all eyes will be on You. Right now I ask that You keep me focused on pleasing You and not on the actual task. Obedience is better than sacrifice so I ask that You keep Obedience at the forefront of everything I do!

In Jesus' name, Amen.

THERE IS POWER IN PRAYER AND OBEDIENCE!

Designate Morning Alone Time With God

DEAR GOD, 41

Spending time with You in the morning has helped me tap into my true purpose for living! For so long, I never really knew what my purpose was and had no idea of where to even begin searching for it. But, the more I read and feed my spirit, it's like You are dropping seed that is growing me.

Now, I can confidently say that *"I have a purpose-driven life"* and with me being fueled by passion and purpose it makes me experience people and interact with them differently than I ever did before. I am proud to say that throughout the day, my experiences and interactions with people are completely different! I look for ways to be a blessing! I look for ways to brighten someone else's day! *This is the new me and I love it!*

I love how others see God in Me. When I am simply being nice and courteous they see You!

I ask in the name of Jesus that You help me to keep this going! Help me to see myself as You see me and help me to no longer be okay with being rude and mean even if that's how others are treating me!

I'm growing and maturing spiritually and You get all the credit for that!

In the name of Jesus that I pray, Amen.

42 DEAR GOD,

Glory to Your Majestic Name! It feels so good to be connected in my heart and connected in my spirit to You. For so long, I knew *of You* God...but I didn't really *know* You! If that even makes sense.

It's like I knew You existed and I knew that I should believe in You from growing up hearing that that's the *right way* to live, but I didn't know *why*!

Oh! But My My! Now, God I see *Why* and the most beautiful thing about that... is that now I see why *"for myself "* without anybody *"forcing"* me to do it! It feels so good that I am growing and maturing spiritually that I desire a personal relationship with You...*on my own!*

I know that the more I seek, the more I will find because Your word says "Ask, and it will be given to you; seek, and you will find; knock, and it will be opened to you. For everyone who asks receives, and he who seeks finds, and to him who knocks it will be opened." (Matthew 7:7-8)

So today, as I spend this morning time with You, help me to remain diligent in my pursuit of spiritual growth.

In the name of Jesus that I pray, Amen.

Designate Morning Alone Time With God

DEAR GOD, 43

Your Word says, "But seek first the kingdom of God and His righteousness, and all these things shall be added to you." (Matthew 6:33) And that's exactly what I'm doing! I'm seeking after You God! The more I learn, the more I will grow…and the more I grow spiritually, the more Joy I will have!

Jesus, I desire to have true Joy! Not just happiness because that is tied into some kind of variable… like "if I have this then I'll be happy" No! I want Joy, so even if I have "*nothing*"…I still have my relationship with You which equates to me still having my Joy!

Jesus, I know that Joy comes through a personal relationship with You! So, this morning and every morning that I *Push Through*…I am molding my mind not to look at my circumstances as they are *now*, but as they *will be* because You are El Shaddai, "You are God-Almighty". Your Omnipotence is powerful enough to supply all I need regardless of what I can see!

So, I ask that You keep me focused on building my relationship with You, so that my life can flow with unmovable, unshakeable Joy!

In Jesus' name, Amen.

44 DEAR GOD,

Hallelujah! Hallelujah! Hallelujah! I used to feel so uncomfortable trying to worship You! But look at how easy it now flows off my tongue!

As I have been spending morning alone time with You, I have learned that "worship" is the gateway to Breakthrough! And it starts with a heart of Surrender!

Thank You, Jesus, because I have learned how to create an atmosphere in my home where I can surrender every thought of worry and replace it with words of Power!

- "Hallelujah to Your Majestic and Glorious name" are words of *Power*.
- "Hallelujah, You are Alpha and Omega… You are the beginning and the end" are words of *Power*.
- "Hallelujah, Great God that You are" are words of *Power*.
- "Hallelujah, Spirit of the living God" are words of *Power*.

So, as I *Push Through* every morning, I will start to incorporate "Worship" into my routine so that I can set the atmosphere for your presence to transform me! I am no longer uncomfortable… I have found my groove!

In Jesus' name, Amen.

Designate Morning Alone Time With God

DEAR GOD, 45

You know how people always say "The Best is Yet to Come"...usually I'm sarcastically like *"yes, sure it is!"* but lately since I have been waking up early to spend time with You, I actually feel confident and believe that!

Yes! The Best *is* Yet to Come, not just for me... but for me *and* my family!

- Holding the title as a wife and being mentally and emotionally strong enough to submit to my husband as being the head and leader of our home, Yes*! "The Best is Yet to Come" for me!*

- Waking up to my husband who absolutely adores me, protects and provides for our family, Yes*! "The Best is Yet to Come" for me!*

- Having a full, happy and peaceful home filled with laughter and love, *Yes! "The Best is Yet to Come" for me!*

- Building financial security and generating wealth for my children's children, *Yes! "The Best is Yet to Come" for me!*

- Living with purpose and feeling fulfilled in my career and business, *Yes! "The Best is Yet to Come" for me!*

I will continue to speak those words out of my mouth, because I'm intentionally backing it by Faith that these things *will* come to pass no matter how my circumstance may look now. God, Your word says "Now faith is the substance of things hoped for, the evidence of things not seen." (Hebrews 11:1) So, By Faith I call these things forth in the name of Jesus and my Faith calls it *Done*!

In Jesus' name, Amen.

GOD IS PREPARING ME FOR SOMETHING NEW!

Designate Morning Alone Time With God

DEAR GOD, 46

I love this new confidence I have in spending time with You! When I first started, I was lost and didn't know what I was doing and it was so uncomfortable. But, even when I didn't know if I was creating a routine or not...I continued to *just try*! Thank You Jesus, because you never let me give up on myself!

I feel *so* good on the inside and I can see how it's overflowing with people around me! I'm not viewed as the "angry woman" anymore, or the "irritated one that nobody can talk to until I've had my coffee." No, I wake up and designate morning alone time with You so by the time I get dressed and leave out of the house... I am Refreshed and feel like a new woman... *That's Growth for Me* and I love it!

I refuse to go back to my old ways, so I ask that You send me people and resources that will keep me motivated and excited for You! Change up my circle of friends so that spiritual growth and maturity can be contagious and that we get excited and feed off of one another's positive energy!

God, I ask that You *elevate* my thinking and everyone I'm connected to!

In the name of Jesus that I pray, Amen.

47 DEAR GOD,

Blessings on Blessings on Blessings, I call them forth In Jesus Name! I know that what You are going to do for me is so much bigger than I can even imagine. I know that the blessing is going to blow my mind!

It feels like it's right around the corner and My God, I can say with excitement and expectation that it was so worth the wait! It was worth me *"Waking Up Early"*, it was worth me changing my habits, it was worth me being obedient; it was so worth me being disciplined.

It's like every piece of the puzzle of my life makes sense to me now!

Thank You Jesus for how You used every situation that I thought would hinder me, set me back or hurt me and use it as a preparation tool to get me ready for the mind blowing blessing that You have for me! Your Word is so true that says, "*It is* good for me that I have been afflicted, that I may learn Your statutes." (Psalm 119:71)

Jesus, because of what I have been through, it pushed me to grow closer and develop a personal relationship with You. Thank You for every tear I shed, that warranted me to be where I am today, which is continuously seeking after You. I am grateful for my Growth!

In Jesus' name, Amen.

Designate Morning Alone Time With God

48

DEAR GOD,

I know I have been anxious in the past. I know I have tried to do it my way before. I know that I didn't always acknowledge You and took credit for things that I shouldn't have. So, this morning I come to You asking for forgiveness. I know that all I have to do is humbly ask for forgiveness *one* time and just like that God, *You have forgiven me.*

So, now I make a declaration to You from this day forward, in the name of Jesus:

- I declare that I *will* wait for the promises to manifest in my life and not try to do it on my own.

- I declare that I *will* continue to trust You for the fullness of Your favor, provision, and overflow.

- I declare that I *will* be obedient the first time that the Holy Spirit nudges me to do something.

These declarations will keep me focused on changing my mindset and with my mindset changing; ultimately the desires of my heart will change too! No longer will my desires be vain and materialistic, but they will be desires that grow the same way I am growing. My desires will be clearer and more spirit-led and also more impactful to others and less self-centered. Oh! Thank You Jesus for my Growth!

In Jesus' name, Amen.

49 DEAR GOD,

I love how strategic You are about my life! Every heartbreak that should have left me depressed and lonely, every part of my background that should have disqualified me and every mistake and bad decision that should have broken me to my core was all a part of *Your* plan!

Every single thing that should have counted me out, You are bringing it all back full circle. The more I designate morning alone time with You; it is making me more confident in speaking wellness over my *life.*

God, I thank You for being Jehovah Rapha, which means *"You are My Healer"*, You have the power to heal me emotionally and physically:

- Emotionally, You are healing my heart from all of the broken relationships that made me feel lesser than as if I am not worthy of love.
- Physically, You are healing me from every disease and attack on my body that tries to attach itself in the form of cancer, lupus, stroke, diabetes, and even the silent killer *stress*!

I decree and I declare in the name of Jesus that, *You are my Healer! You are my Healer!... You...Are...My...Healer* and the continuous worry behind every attack of the enemy *stops* today! Worry and Stress you no longer have control over my mind, because I have the authority to *speak* to you and *command* you to *Cease!* In Jesus' name.

It's in the name of Jesus that I pray, Amen.

Designate Morning Alone Time With God

50

DEAR GOD,

Thank You in advance for the groundbreaking blessing that will completely blow my mind and change my life!

God, I'm sitting here thinking about all of the years that I prayed and thought they were being ignored or falling on deaf ears. Oh! But My God! All that time was for this moment, where the Breakthrough is right around the corner! I am so excited about it but even amid my excitement... I must pause and ask for the Holy Spirit to help me.

Oh! Holy Spirit, keep me focused not on the blessing but everything I did to prepare myself *for* the blessing. I prepared myself by finally choosing to restore my personal relationship with God. Help me to remember how I got to this point and that was by waking up early to spend time with You, reading my bible for understanding, truth, and knowledge, praying with boldness and authority, worshiping with humility and writing in my prayer journal with transparency and vulnerability. All these things combined helped me build the spiritual foundation needed to handle living the "Blessed Life!"

Ah! *"The Blessed Life"* that even sounds good rolling off my tongue! I love You God and if I haven't said it enough... I want You to know that I am truly grateful for everything!

I know that this is *still* just the beginning...so please keep my heart open and focused on You!

In the name of Jesus that I pray, Amen.

LET'S STAY CONNECTED!

For more resources, bookings, and speaking inquiries visit:

www.shantiacoleman.com

For questions, comments, feedback, and reviews email:

coach@shantiacoleman.com

For daily encouragement and inspiration follow:

@shantiacoleman

BOOKS BY SHANTIA

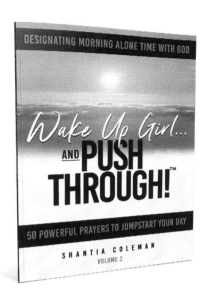

Wake Up Girl... and PUSH Through!®
Volume 2

Wake Up Man... and PUSH Through!®
Men's Edition

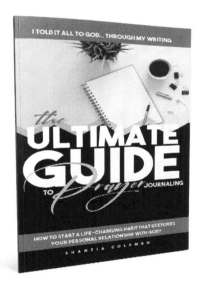

The Ultimate Guide to Prayer Journaling

Available online at www.shantiacoleman.com